IN CABAZON

IN CABAZON

Trevor Losh-Johnson

Artwork by

Ken Johnson

BlankSpace Publications

In Cabazon

ISBN 978-0-9732980-3-1

First Edition.
First Printing October 2012.

Printed and bound in Canada at McMaster University, Hamilton,
Ontario.

McMaster University Innovation Press
McMaster University GH-B101
1280 Main Street West
Hamilton, ON, L8S 4L8
Canada

BlankSpace Publications
www.blankspacepub.com

to Jocelyn, in memory of Robert Dewey

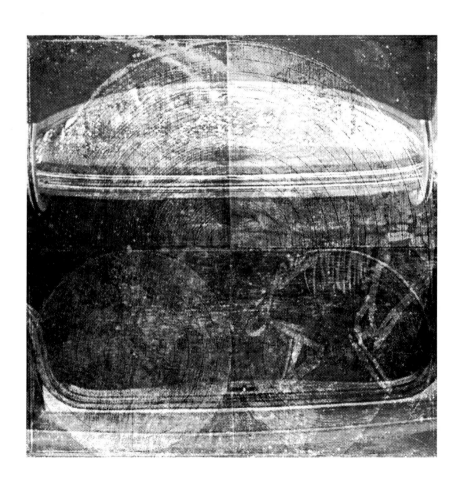

1. Pre.

This book will prepare you to argue against idolatrous museums.

It is for the child who, walking through a darkened house, glimpsing through broad glass and seeing a mooncolored, draped shape in the backyard, cannot think to call out but hides beneath familiar covers.

It is of and for Californian deserts.

This is the art of memory:

2.i.

I will neglect
        the fields I own
and build a church in Cabazon.

There are more fertile worlds grown
than vines, fleshy fruits, or grains

I will exchange
        dingy rains
for a river hemmed by unbounded plains:

3.ii.

For the forest scrubbed by the vessel and flame
We look to the ornamental East
From our city deluged by the cloudbank's flare
That receding left a bowl of disease

I hope that renascent frosts will melt
That smother the nesting birds each spring
And what was residue, webs of mold
Will evanesce from all goldwrought things

4.iii.

For it was you who made me king
And love your starling's cloud of kin
Manning me with a spade and a knife

And brought me the swamp interring the dead
To display one child alive and dazed
Standing beside me, my queentree of life

5. ii.

Felix filled the tank of his tan sedan.

He ignited his engine but left it running, remembering to scrub his marked windshield.

The storm clouds were moving east, along with him, but sunsplashes spread across the chaparral.

Felix sponged the dirtstains from the rain off the glass and glanced at a man lingering by the station's doors.

He returned stumbling into his seat and wiped eggwhite from his cheeks and his nose.

Turning right onto the road, he saw an indigo coupe in the lot across the street, signaling left.

When the street cleared, Felix began to turn and the indigo coupe lurched left, cutting him off.

Pausing then continuing, Felix merged right and then into the web of freeway traffic.

The clouds above San Bernardino were melting into the blue.

6. iii.

Turning off the freeway, Felix took the Pepper Ave exit and drove around the hospital and the King of King's Cemetery, Colton.

He found his way back down to H Street, and he turned to park across the street from number 528, a gabled Victorian house with bay windows and its roof stippled with stone teardrops.

Felix approached the door, and saw the stone pearls fly away, small birds united in a tangle.
Some alighted on a mammoth tv antenna.
Laundry hung on a line and on the front fence.
Felix knocked, and a haltering woman finally arrived.
He asked if Mia was staying here.

If not, he countered, had she continued to her brother's at Palm Springs?
Her aunt shook her head.

Crossing the yard as he left, Felix tripped over a sprinklerhead and his foot sank into a flooded patch of grass.

With the inside of his car door and floormat smeared with mud he drove back towards the freeway.

7. iii.

Without my own all houses are strange
   and are a yarn knot of roads
And there are no names on smooth stones
   in graven, indexed rows
Her laughing voice could melt beneath the snows
If no one spoke again her name
   then every word
   is spoken blurred
And immaculate as tropic waning floes

Stand with me though
   and be my love
And we will all the outworld probe

8.i.

I will delimit
    This liquid space
And find the contours of her face

But if I cannot peer through those eyes
I pray that they will lift at sunrise

Find tumbling worlds engulfing my own
Where I will stand
        still in Cabazon

9. ii.

Voyagers for the pleasures of the travels
Expend their sole possessions vaporous as contrails
That shorn propel them to a purer time
Arrange the mucked din to a consonant tone

Then voices there must shine from a unit breath
And every fresh astonishing meeting both
                    One I have known
                    And advent of the new

10. i.

But do not let the mocked age and sheen
                        biologism
                        chronic loss
Of makeup let you think it more than screen

That is not hair you mingle with your own
That is Fiona
                Mannequined fluorescence

Harlot of churches

It is kneeling to the floor and finding none
                The end of concupiscence

11. ii.

May the desert's bowl lie flat and clean on the earth's ball
No more bodies scattered there or scooped

Before there were only to tempt a fall
The slither and hiss immingled in wind
And now the hurlevent
                screech of flying drones
                response and caul

Let me shed my sinful skin
And tear the unwound binding cloak
Standing nakedfresh in a sunspotted clear
                and dive within

12. ii.

Following the freeway, Felix balanced between his knees a cup of ice cream, a flat wooden spoon, and a plastic bottle of soda.

He fished in his pocket for a phone, and looked toward the hill and emerging mountain ridges.

Through the windows of neighboring cars he would perceive Mia's face and blink, tempted to honk, wave, or call out.

He nearly hurled his phone through another window when he saw her in her posture.

But, thinking again, he sent instead a text to Fiona and wound up his window to guard against the shiver and hiss of wind.

Mia's apparitions were flickeringly projected, and stopped with Fiona's phone call.

Text received, no I have not seen Mia—I am in Redlands, and would you like to stop to talk about it?

Let me take the turnoff—no, don't clean up I can only stop for a short time.
The cars beside him flinched.

She said she had been crying and would like to unwind with a friend, and to help back.

But I cannot stay, I am bound for Palm Springs unless you or any of her cousins heard from her here.

Well we'll talk about it—come to that divebar where we met once back then.
We'll see you soon.

13. iii.

He had not stopped by Redlands in years, and the streets here were unfamiliar.
Some took him at angles he did not expect.
They twisted and knotted and the rows of houses in suburban plots dizzied him.
At last he passed a familiar signpost, parked, and walked to the door of the bar Fiona dictated.
There were times when he and Mia would drive past there without pausing.
He stopped at her laugh.
He felt her hand beneath his own.
She did not stop walking and pulled him chirping away from the door.
They spoke many words reminiscing.
Why were you sad?
I am not anymore now that you're here—where's your wife?
A quarrel, and she left from me—going towards Palm Springs.
She fixed him in her stare, and said how joyful, joyful she was now to see him.
And how warm he felt, the dress she was wearing filling him with the calm of memories, as her hips filled it, by the way it flowed.
He stood with her by the East State Street curb.
She played her knuckles over the wrinkles of his shirt.
Their lips turned and merged.

14. i.

A prayer for the faith of Felix—
On the composition of the diploid cathedral and its root—
Those who have not will mock those who have seen it.
He shall be arrested and copied endlessly.
From the femur of Cro Magnon to his flickering screen,
the Cathedral at Cabazon welcomes all who enter—we have not
made it up.
It is in the desert that you may fill its architraves, and in a
chapel you may see its print.
It contains and is imprinted on all grains.
But beware hollow sanctuaries and surfaceskinned
automatons, and palefalse prophets of the sun.
It falls to correct and it stands.
The cathedral's trace is in every grain.
The sanctuary is cavernous, the carnivorous minaret near.
She contains in her leviathan's belly the phoebian
treeseed tablets with which he sows his golden grains.
They stand apart.
Return Felix to kneel at the grounds.
Meet at the oasis the Kanche and Piscis.
Aman.

15.iii.

I melted in a maze of my entrails

16.i.

A voice called out of the whirlwind

       Of the god that lays all layers
              crepuscule and stone
              epigene and histone
     Into a paletted rainbowflare

It spoke and of its own, rapacious heart
          it ate and swallowed
        I sought fallowed
     To try and cast off every part

And did I know of the bovine earth its molten core?
And could I draw aside the sea's curtain?

For given a span beyond the powers of counting
I could not catch the fish or hold the conch.

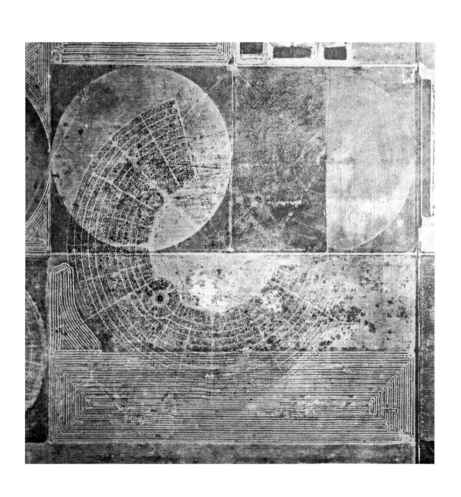

Felix's phone rang and he fumbled in his pocket and Fiona asked him if he wanted her to answer it for him since he was driving.

It was Mia's number but when he answered nobody spoke.

The call disconnected itself.

The sun sinking behind them cast separate colors in the sky and they melded into the rocks of the mountains beside them.

He cursed his fluttering heart that he had kissed Fiona even in greeting and the hateful prospect that she might think he would exchange a wife and unborn child for a trifling, old romance.

She played her painted nails over his thigh and he swallowed.

Why is she angry at you, she asked.

Though it angered him that he would conceive of confiding he spoke it anyway, and said that Mia was pregnant and he had told her it would do better to get rid of it.

He'd repented of that, but she had already left their apartment after tears.

Fiona said she was sorry, softened her grip, and then asked where he would go if she was not in Palm Springs?

She could be anywhere around the earth for all he knew.

Why not look for a grape in wine?

It would rather be like finding one fish in the populous sea.

That's funny, she said, and added that if this turned out badly he could stay with her for as long as he needed.

He apologized for picking her up and for having involved her before anything was resolved.

I'd better take you home, now.

She dangled her hand out the window.

An indigo coupe merged into Felix's rearview mirror.

His phone again rang and he found it once more in his pocket.
It was Mia's number but no voice spoke before its disconnection.
  I don't think you wanted to see me said Fiona with hard
tones while Felix watched his rearview mirror.
The coupe lurched behind him and he accelerated.
It happened again and he honked his horn.
  He's an angry kid, maybe he wants to pass you, Fiona
murmured, and Felix changed lanes.
He gestured out of his window.
  The coupe merged behind him again, and Felix saw the
sawtooth band of the driver's yellow hat.
  Fiona, agitated, suggested he pull off the freeway and
Mia's number called his phone.
He could not answer, and agreed they should stop.
  She began to wind her window up as he turned off the
thin Morongo exit past Johnson Lane but stopped to point for
him to enter the roundabout and he turned from the mountains
while the wind hissed.
They drove through the second roundabout.
  A tower appeared and they veered left and entered its
parking lot, winding through it towards the tower.
  Felix asked if they could turn around, that he was sure
they had lost the coupe at the turnoff.
Let's park, she replied, and rest briefly before we leave.
I will take you back to Redlands.
No no, she said, you can keep going towards Palm Springs,
I don't live in Redlands,
  I was driving towards Palm Springs when you called,
  Let's stop and go into the casino, they have a nice pool
beside it—surely we can talk there—
Don't be too hard on yourself—things could be worse.

19.iii.

It was dusk and beyond, and the way through the lot was dim.

They wove through and Felix asked which way back to the entrance but Fiona insisted they park.

They spun about in a maze of spaces yet he turned towards the exit.

He pushed towards where they had entered, and found themselves at the westwardly, third roundabout where there were no spaces.

She demanded he park, Felix complied, and she jolted her door and stepped suddenly out, in the red.
He followed.

She was walking to spaces opposite from his and she stopped, by the one other car parked illegally in the circle, the indigo coupe.

They exited the sedan and stood bounded by steep, sharp rockcovered slopes.
The yellowbrimmed man stood beside his coupe.
Felix froze and they crossed again to his tan sedan.

He is going to gut you Fiona said.

The yellowbrimmed man, young but jaggedly gaunt, took a straight razor from his pants and opened it.
He sliced it at Felix's stomach.
Felix leaped back and cried confusion.
There were no others near in the lot.

Felix ran to his sedan and was opening the door as the man stooped and with an icepick in his other hand stabbed suddenly his tire.
Fiona was laughing.
She shrieked and she cried.
Felix screamasked who he was, why she did all this.

The man grabbed him and held his arm with his razor drawn back.

Fiona tore the abdomen of her blouse open and shrieked this is what you had wanted me to cut when I didn't—his name is Marlowe.
He is my son.

Daddy said the grinning man, who had whiskers and rancid teeth.

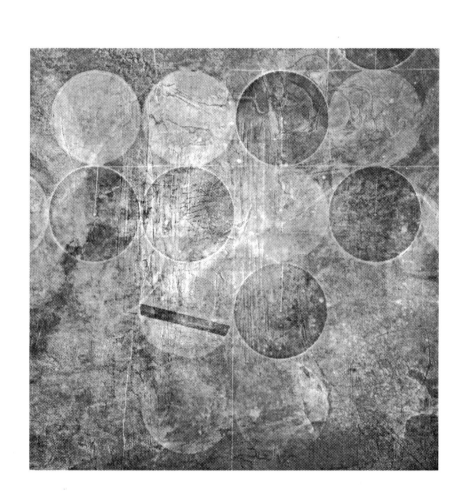

20.ii.

      Felix found himself sprinting past Fiona and Marlowe, who bent down to regain the razor and the hat Felix knocked from his head.

      Fiona began screaming catch him, and Felix saw he could not cross on foot the mounds of rock beyond the coupe.

      Finding that Marlowe had left the keys in the ignition and left the motor running, Felix fumbled with the door and it was open.

      Before Marlowe could reach him through the open window he managed to shift the automatic transmission and maneuver the squealing tires away from the two and after turns and turns left the parkinglot.

      The roundabout he encountered first confused him and he turned on the northern road parallel to the freeway.

      He drove fast and east and entered the next parking lot two miles away from the last, away from the tower and pool high behind him.

      He plunged into the lot above the first building and sat alone, lights off, breathing sharply in the dark.

Behind him, on a polished seat, a heap of clothes began chanting his name.

It was his voice.

Mia had asked him to speak his name for her ringtone.

He found her phone in three heaps of what could have been her clothes.

The pile was clean.

He did not call the police, he could not think to explain his car.

Leaving it and clutching Mia's phone, he walked to the steps of the inn between the Burger King and Shell station and thought to ask for help but repented.

He read the printed menu in the window.

His stomach was empty and perhaps all he saw was a misunderstanding and to eat would restore his car and negate her phone from his hand and he reached to his pocket to count his cash.

His wallet was in his glove box, he recalled.

Returning, lilting slightly, he saw the parked indigo coupe.

He had left its keys in the ignition.

He started to sob, and recalled that if anything had happened to Mia her phone was in his hand and the clothes she may have worn in the back of the car he was driving.

Her aunt saw him pursuing her.

Perhaps they would check the car's registration if they did not think he stole it.

He searched for a space capacious enough to hide her clothes until he thought it all out.

He took the keys, shut the door, and opened the back to scoop up the clothes to place into the trunk.

The ignition key clicked in the lock.

When he opened the trunk he saw the bundle and reached in to feel something damp.

The icebody in the dark was large enough to be her own.

The spongy ropes in his hand were not ropes.

Pushing his whole self away, he vomited into the air.

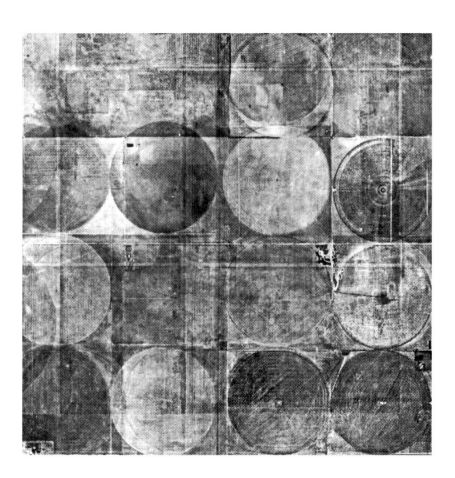

22.iii.

The chronic encyclical or the endless desert dream
Bound in raiment my seven severed parts

I have known three labyrinths

        the tangled rose
           and its budding heart

        the fire conducting
           smoke from the hill

And darkness without form or lighted means

When everything must eat and all must kill
    The wick is out

    To eat disgorged of earth and sky and vaults

We do not pass on
We are passed by

23.i

The sun dropped
My face upon the tide
Rippled into darkness and the gulf

My hands dipped
Probing in the deep
Amid lurking faces, scaled sides

We came upon a holy place
Where irisflared fins steep
In sun and at a wineclothed chaos
Beams retreat and stop

Holy of Holies
      Curled life in a seashell case

24.ii.

Who am I to proffer what I have culled
And prepare my deeds before an Osiric Lord
Who shall lay my heart upon the scales in scorn
And tell me rise if it be vaporous and light

Shall I enter every spirit that received me
Misunderstand my meaning or feel pain
And shrinking from that behemoth I was
Repent I were not single as the palm

Infinities of misdeeds as the rain
Cast under cloaked clouds and all call down
Rings and thunderous wind my sinful name
That plucked one Lord discarded forgot and damned

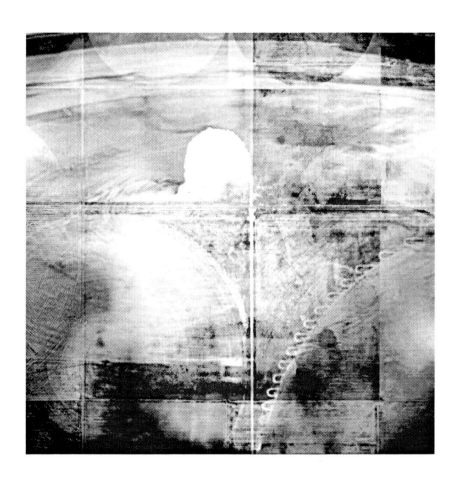

25.i.

In nightshades by gashwork her face had been denuded of features.
Felix squinted into the trunk to search for other signs.
Her fingers were stripped, but the height and softness of the unclotted hair correct.
He felt her face and there was the smooth touch of bone.
He made sounds he did not recognize as correct.
Again he stood erect by the open trunk.
She had been opened and fell into darkness.
Fiona had plotted, Marlowe had cut, or she joined him.
Where was she while he drove alongside Fiona?
The trunk was behind him since Colton.
How long had he stood beside her while there was light he had kindled and beams in her unknown?
He stared into her stomach for a childform and could see nothing but lipflared shapes like frozen flowing water.
Could there be teeth layered rancid in the womb?
Every round part was spread out.
Blackblood reflected pinpoints of floodlight.
Felix shut the trunk.

Felix drove yards to the gas station and chanced witnesses on counters to buy gas and water bottles with cash.

He emptied the bottles beneath the car and filled them after the tank.

Winding down the window to hear all sounds he turned right on Seminole Dr. towards the casino tower and combed the parking lot for his car.

Neither it nor Fiona was to be seen in any row.

Orienting himself he drove back briefly east and turned up an umbral dirt path beneath a lighted billboard, drove up and parked at a crosstrail beyond a low fence in the pitch leading back to the casino.

He did not bear opening the trunk again.

He splashed gas underneath and in the car.

Choking on the vapors he saw his fingertips were black in the moonlight.

By the lit lighter they were red.

He wiped his palms inside his coat and divested of it touched the cloth with flame.

His hands appeared clean in the periglow.

He tossed the torch underneath the car.

After climbing and clearing a fence and running under a line of patriarchal telephone poles towards the casino's busport, he looked back behind.

Flames were burning out the shell and a pillar of smoke rose towards the clouds.

He prayed for the blackcake clouds to withhold their rain and for the sloped winds down the mountains to subside.

27.ii.

In the desert rock is the gemlike flame
That pillows in calciform snow what lived
      Pompey kept its beecomb frame
Or else it dissipates in smoke

Smoke on the rock a wisp and a film
Mia rained on Cabazon
No portrait can paint, no fossil frame
The child's laughter we breathed and drank

28.iii.

Marlowe is a ratio

Among three pageants I sought a face
in the temple its type
in the crowd its kind
in all others its lack

Expected the fish when it breached to be sunned

But found its farce when the knot unwound

In a foreign city her name among tongues
Excreted from me punned

Marlowe is the beaching of Leviathan's rind
And counting each grain of the rotten mound

29.i.

At the Cabazon museum a single room
Contained two antechambers, sun and moon
And I took the latter through a purple veil
Silent and dim the chamber led past a mural
As on a cave's wall down unintended steps
A plesiosaur suspended in the deep
Caught a darting fish with needleteeth
And past the mural encased upon the wall
A fossilfrieze of curled bones in rock
As boulders pebble the surface of shallow lakes
And diagrammed beside the osseous heap
A map depicting how the mother lay
And where to note the bones in the uterine wall
Beside that broken eggs or stomach stones

30.iii.

In the oilhot temple smells of olive and cedar
Climb along the columns to erect
The prehistoric past with carved dinonecks
Inhabited of old Titans, serpentine and follicular
Those cornices seethed and the room suffused with green
And while the herd milled like scattered palms
A pack, bipedal carnivores, lurked and surveyed
At once took casually the nearest calf
And exerted after others but the mothers
Trampled many—one both dazed and hurt
Pressed its snout to its partner's neck and found
Gashes and spongiform tissue—ponderously
Their knees sank beneath buckling weights to the mud
And let the carcasses rot in the fetid place

31.i.

A newday ark to preserve all that would die
                seedpods stored in a polar vault
                tigers walking in the snow
          Museums to constitute gone days

I walked above, between two tanks
                splashing formaldehyde
An oarfish floating in one, its double a sunflower
Both lost all color and were sable when they died

I looked above for a rainbow in air
                      or archangel

If the rocks do not stand
When the tide caves the beach in
We will preserve them
                however peregrine

Send loose two birds to find a higher point
Fixed and holy
Where to plant our legs
And build our church
And the cosmogone egg

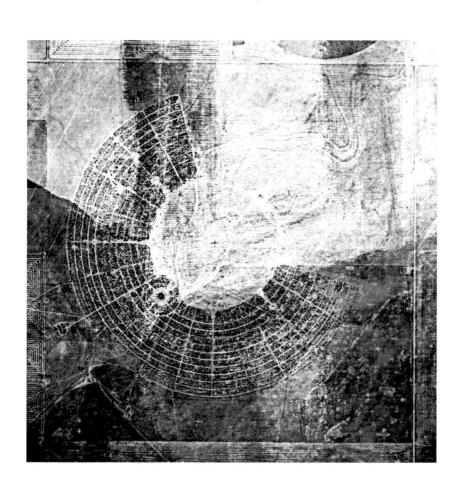

32. Post.

You will then remember

        from forking Janus to Death's ember

        One body of amalgamated worlds

                in the eddies

           still and curled

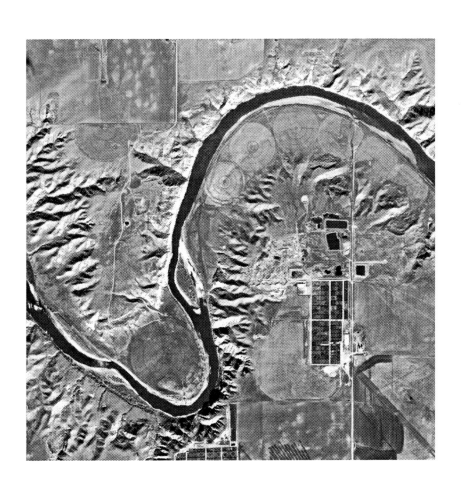

Trevor Losh-Johnson lives in a small college town in Southern California, beneath the hills that border the San Gabriel Mountain Range. This region of America is susceptible to earthquakes and fires. *In Cabazon* is his first book.

Ken Johnson lives in that same Californian college town, painting, photographing, teaching, and generally trying to make sense of things. In addition to exhibiting work throughout his native United States, he has been exhibited internationally in Australia and Canada, and is a member of the Society of Layerists in Multimedia.